barbecue

barbecue

CLARE FERGUSON

CASTLE BOOKS

This edition published in 2011 by
CASTLE BOOKS (R)
a division of BOOK SALES, INC.
276 Fifth Avenue Suite 206
New York, New York 10001
USA

This edition published by arrangement with Jacqui Small, an
imprint of Aurum Press Limited, 7 Greenland St, London, NW1 0ND

First published in 2007 by Jacqui Small

Publisher   Jacqui Small
Editorial manager   Kate John
Art Director   Ashley Western
Photography   Jeremy Hopley and Martin Brigdale
Editor   Madeline Weston
Production   Peter Colley

ISBN-13: 978-0-7858-2762-7

10 9 8 7 6 5 4 3 2 1

Printed in China

contents

INTRODUCTION

Many of my happiest childhood memories involve food, drink and driftwood fires out of doors. Such activities still delight me: fresh air makes our eyes sparkle, gives edge to our appetites, gets our hearts racing.

Barbecues, by their very nature, involve primal sensations: heat, light, the gorgeous smell of sizzling snacks. While the charcoal progresses from sparks and flames to a steady ash-covered glow (the correct stage to barbecue) we can assemble ingredients, break bread, mix a dressing, pour drinks, hand out nibbles. Some people may admire the view, take a wander, bounce a ball, gather berries, paddle in the surf, or strum a guitar. Being away from our usual preoccupations means feeling part of a wider world than that of the kitchen and dining table ... enjoying intriguing hot, hissing sounds and the intense tastes of freshly cooked foods.

Picnicking and barbecuing are democratic activities. Tiny tots can gather flat stones, grandparents arrange driftwood piles, laconic teens and shy guests uncork wine, toss salads. Husbands or lovers may excel at mixing cocktails or marinating the chicken. Aunties can help by arranging umbrellas and cushions. Laughter, story-telling, charades, volleyball, are often enjoyable outcomes of time spent around the barbecue. Inhibitions vanish and we relax. Autumn or spring barbecues, perfect times for natural foraging (blackberries, hazelnuts, fairy-ring or cep mushrooms, wild garlic leaves) may be just as successful as summer ones. Even winter barbecues can be exhilarating with tented shelters and vacuum flasks of hot soup or mulled wine.

Sand in the sandwiches, slugs in the salad, lukewarm champagne and charred sausages are a thing of the past: today's barbecue-givers and party-lovers enjoy simplicity and easy, often ethnic, foods as well as interesting drinks. Disasters can be avoided with a bit of clever planning.

Meat, fish or poultry brochettes in their basic state; ready-made marinades, dressings and toppings to add on site; crusty fresh bread, fresh fruits, seasonal fresh vegetables; local pastry specialties, regional cheeses: these typify a successful barbecue menu. And not everything needs to be cooked: raw can be best.

Now that multi-cultural weekday meals are the norm (tzatziki, crudités, chilli con carne, mousse) there's every reason to enjoy French-style radishes, bruschetta, game burgers then Munster cheese with pears. Throw away the rule book: let creativity flourish. Barbecues can provide real gaiety whether they take place in the back garden, on a roof terrace, beside river, lake or beach or during a school fête. Lift your spirits and have some convivial, *al fresco* fun with family and friends.

EQUIPMENT

Enjoyable barbecues don't necessarily require costly, complicated gear. Plastic hampers and insulated cool boxes work just as well as wicker-work hampers and silver ice buckets. Cardboard bottle carriers do the same job as the antique metal variety. Foil-tray disposables or a galvanised iron fold-up barbecue or a handsome French iron barbecue racks with legs and a handle can work just as efficiently as a glamorous domed chrome and enamel gas-fired contraption (though for certain ambitious events and situations, these barbecues are excellent too). Even a few stones or bricks and a grill rack can suffice. Absolute essentials are wood or metal barbecue skewers and some kitchen foil, kitchen scissors and a sharp serrated knife.

Methodical organisers often include umbrellas, waterproof groundsheets, rugs, cushions and insect-repellent candles or flares. They know that easy-to-operate gear, tongs, appropriate fuel, a corkscrew, bottle opener, well stacked china, cutlery and glasses and some kitchen paper on a roll are essential needs. Take rubbish bags: littering is antisocial. Buy mineral water, bags of ice along with fresh juice, wines, beers and other temperature-sensitive items near to your destination if you have little in the way of insulated containers.

Supermarkets and petrol stations, home-supply stores, delicatessens, ethnic grocers, wayside stalls and farmers markets can provide food and drink essentials as well as useful tools.

1 A large galvanised metal barbecue can be found in Greek shops. The rack folds back to cook kebabs.
2 A lightweight camping stool can double up as a table and is easy to carry.
3 At dusk, a pressure lamp and lanterns will light your feast. Citronella candles will keep mosquitoes at bay.
4 A windproof camping gas stove and a lightweight kettle mean you can have a cup of tea anywhere.
5 Stainless steel cutlery may be heavier but it is a pleasure to use. Bowls and buckets are useful for salads and rice. 6 Other useful items include a penknife, can opener, tongs, oyster knife, corkscrew, camping plates and wooden spoons.

STARTERS & SOUPS

carrot, orange & cardamom soup

An exotic, vivid, colourful and fragrant soup that can be made in a flash. Serve it hot or iced. The harissa, a red, spicy North African condiment, is delicious when home made (see page 43) and is also available from French and African stores, and good delis and supermarkets.

1 Peel and thinly slice the carrots crosswise into a small saucepan. Add the hot stock, bring to boiling, and reduce to a lively simmer.

2 Add the salt, harissa and black cardamom seeds removed from their green pods. Stir to mix. Squeeze in the juice of the oranges. Use a grater or zester to remove ¼-½ teaspoon of orange zest.

3 When the carrots are tender, 10-12 minutes, pour the pan contents plus the zest and shallot into a blender. Blend to a creamy soup.

4 Heat to boiling, or chill thoroughly. Pour the soup into a vacuum flask and seal. Wrap up the extra cardamom pods and take along as well.

5 Serve in bowls, cups, demitasse cups or glasses. Savour the aroma, scattering on some extra cardamom seeds for pleasure just before drinking.

Makes 5 cups (1.2 litres), Serves 4

Ingredients
1¼ lb (500g) large organic carrots
3 cups (750ml) chicken or vegetable stock, boiling
½ teaspoon sea salt flakes
1-2 teaspoons harissa (hot spicy) paste
20 green cardamom pods, crushed, plus 8 to garnish
2 oranges, scrubbed
1 small shallot, finely chopped

iced black bean soup with chipotle cream

A Mexican-style soup and a beauty - the perfect starter for a summer barbecue. If authentic dried black beans (not Chinese salted black beans) are hard to find, substitute several cans of good quality black beans: this saves hours. An ethnic grocer, deli or spice stall will stock essential ingredients.

1 Heat the oil, add the scallions (spring onions) and sauté 2-3 minutes. Add the garlic, green jalapeño, cumin, ground and fresh cilantro (coriander), tomato purée and beans. Pour in the boiling stock. Bring the pan contents back to boiling. Simmer, uncovered, for 15 minutes or so.

2 Blend the soup, in batches if necessary, until creamy. Return the soup to the pan. Stir, adjust seasonings and turn off the heat. Cool the soup over iced water. Chill in the refrigerator.

2 Make the chipotle cream: if using chipotles *en escabèche*, simply chop or mash. If using dried chipotles, dry roast them briefly in a hot frying pan then soak briefly in hot water, simmer until soft, then chop or mash.

4 Stir into the cream and pack separately. When the soup is cold, pour into one or two wide-mouthed vacuum flasks, adding 2 ice cubes to each. At serving time, stir the chipotle cream into the soup.

Makes $6\frac{1}{4}$ cups (1.5 litres) , Serves 8

Ingredients

4 tablespoons corn oil
8 scallions (spring onions), chopped
4 garlic cloves, crushed
1 green jalapeño chilli, cored, deseeded, sliced
1 teaspoon ground cumin
2 teaspoons ground coriander
3 oz (75g) fresh cilantro (coriander), chopped
2 tablespoons tomato purée
1 lb 10 oz (750g) cooked or canned black beans
   (*frijoles negros*)
3 cups (750ml) boiling chicken stock
sea salt and freshly ground black pepper

To serve:
2 tablespoons chipotles *en escabèche*, or dried
   chipotles (smoked, dried jalapeños)
$\frac{1}{2}$ cup (150ml) heavy (thick) cream

parmesan & poppy seed palmiers

These pretty, curlicued pastries are a savoury version of the classic sweet ones. Paradoxically, they taste good dusted with icing sugar at serving time. To carry them, pack them into a napkin-lined box or shallow basket.

Makes 32-36

Ingredients
1 lb 10 oz (750g) bought puff pastry in the block
  (or pre-rolled)
4 tablespoons Dijon mustard
4 tablespoons blue poppy seeds
4 tablespoons grated Parmesan cheese (from the block)
2 tablespoons confectioners' (icing) sugar

1 Roll out or unfold the chilled pastry into a rectangle about 8 x 28 in (20 x 70cm), and about $\frac{1}{8}$ in (3mm) thick. Trim the edges. Spread the pastry first with mustard, then poppy seeds, then cheese. Starting from both short sides, roll each in tightly towards the centre so that they meet in a double roll with a 'ram's horn' appearance.

2 Turn the double roll over so that the flat side is up. Using a long, serrated knife and pressing firmly, slice down, crosswise, to give 32-36 slim palmiers.

3 Water spray, or wet by hand, 4 or more baking sheets and lay the palmiers on them, allowing space between each. Chill for 1 hour.

4 Bake 2 sheets at a time in an oven preheated to 450°F (230°C) for 6-7 minutes or until they start to caramelise underneath. With a fish slice, carefully turn each palmier over. Bake again for a further 4-5 minutes or until crispy and caramelised.

5 Repeat with the remaining palmiers until they are all cooked. Cool completely on wire racks. Store in an airtight container for up to 7 days.

6 At serving time, dust them lightly with confectioners' (icing) sugar, using a fine sieve.

radishes, french style

Select beautiful radish specimens: crimson or pink and white, in fat bunches, leaves intact. Choose lovely butter, maybe French *Echiré* (which comes, conveniently, in tiny wooden pails containing 9 oz/250g) and Maldon sea salt.

Serves 4

Ingredients
2-3 bunches fresh, crisp radishes with leaves
unsalted or lightly salted butter, e.g. *Echiré*
$\frac{1}{4}$ cup (50g) Maldon sea salt flakes, *sel du mer* or
  kosher salt

To serve, have the washed, chilled radishes in a cloth-lined basket or box with the (room temperature) butter still in its pail, if possible, and a lidded small pot of salt. Encourage your companions to break off a radish, dunk in butter, dip in salt, eat.

Note:
Some Poilâne or other good sourdough bread might be a nice accompaniment.

hummus

Makes about 1½ lb (700g)

Ingredients

1¼ lb (500g) freshly cooked or
canned chickpeas (about 8 oz/
225g, if cooked from dry)
3 tablespoons tahini (toasted
sesame seed paste)
4 tablespoons freshly squeezed
lemon juice
4 garlic cloves, crushed
¾ teaspoon salt
½ cup (125ml) extra-virgin olive oil

To serve:
Paprika, flatleaf parsley, optional
flatbreads

1 Drain the chickpeas but reserve
some of the liquid. Put them into a
food processor with the tahini, juice,
garlic and salt. Process in several
long bursts to a gritty paste.

2 With the machine running, drizzle
in 7 tbsp (110ml) of the olive oil
through the feed tube until you
have a thick, creamy purée. Do not
over-process – a little roughness is
good. If it seems too dense, process
again, in brief bursts, adding 6-8
tablespoons of cooking liquid.

3 Serve the hummus cool, straight
away, or chill it if it is to be used at a
later time: it keeps well, in the
refrigerator, for up to 1 week.

4 Serve with the reserved olive oil
drizzled over the hummus in its
bowl, a pinch of paprika and some
parsley sprigs, adding warmed torn
flatbreads as needed.

rosita's guacamole

Makes 14 oz (400g) or 6-8 servings

Ingredients

1 medium white, or 1 small Spanish,
onion, chopped
5 oz (150g) bunch fresh cilantro
(coriander) leaves
2 teaspoons sea salt or kosher salt
4 garlic cloves, crushed
4 ripe Hass avocados
2 limes, halved, to garnish (optional)
2 green and 1 red chilli, sliced
½ teaspoon dried oregano (optional)
2 plum tomatoes, cut in 1cm cubes

To serve:
Tostaditas, tortilla crisps, warmed
tortillas, torn

1 Using a big *molcahete* (Mexican
mortar) or big mortar and pestle (or,
less satisfactorily, a food-processor),
combine the onion, cilantro
(coriander), salt and garlic and
pound and mash, or process in brief
bursts, to a green aromatic paste.

2 Scoop in the avocado flesh. Add a
squeeze of fresh lime, if you like and
the green chillies. Stir, pound, mix or
process briefly again.

3 Crumble the oregano on top, if
using. Decorate with a tumble of
red jewel-like tomato cubes and
red chillies.

4 Serve in the *molcahete* or mortar
or a bowl surrounded by the lime
halves and the tostaditas, crisps and
torn tortilla bits.

salsa

Makes about 1⅔ cups (400ml)

Ingredients

1 red onion, finely chopped
3 plum or vine tomatoes, finely
cubed
2 hot fresh red or green chillies,
deseeded, deveined and chopped
juice of 2 limes or 1 lemon
(5-6 tablespoons)
2 tablespoons stock or water
sea salt flakes and crushed
allspice, to taste
1 handful fresh cilantro (coriander),
mint, parsley, chives or thyme, or
a mix, chopped

Combine the ingredients in a non-
reactive bowl, stirring. Taste, adjust
seasonings as needed. Use the same
day. Serve in small or large bowls.

Variations

Substitute 3 scallions (spring
onions) for the red onion.

Substitute blanched, dehusked
tomatillos, or green tomatoes, for
the red tomatoes.

Add 1 teaspoon finely shredded
fresh root ginger and black pepper
instead of allspice and use all
cilantro (coriander), for an Asian-
style salsa.

Add 3-4 tablespoons of extra-virgin
olive oil for a richer effect.

blini with taramasalata & 'saviar'

Blini are yeast-risen pancakes, Russian in origin. This recipe makes 48, so freeze what you don't need for another occasion. Taramasalata, a Greek classic, should be made using pressed, salted cod's roe from a Greek deli. Substitute some salted, smoked cod's roe if none can be found.

Blini method

1 Sift together the flours, yeast and salt in a large heatproof bowl. Add the milk, soured cream and egg yolks, and lightly beat together to make a thick batter. Cover using a large plastic bag. Set on a rack over hand-hot water, not touching the bowl, or in another warm place. Leave for 40-50 minutes or until risen.

2 Whisk the egg whites to a stiff foam and fold in carefully.

3 Preheat a large griddle, hot plate, non-stick or cast iron frying pan. Add 1 tablespoon butter or olive oil. Spoon 8 dessert-spoonfuls of batter, from the tip of a spoon, to make small pancakes. Once the batter sets and bubbles show on the upper surface, turn them over and cook again, briefly, until golden on the second side. Test one: it should be cooked right through.

4 Cook the remaining batter in batches in more hot butter or olive oil. Cool on wire racks.

Taramasalata method

1 Put the tarama or smoked cod's roe into a food-processor with the wet, crumbled bread, the garlic and juice of half the lemon. Process briefly until mixed.

2 With the machine running, drizzle in the oil, in a thin, fine stream until the mixture stiffens into a dense paste. Scrape down the sides as necessary.

3 Drizzle in 3-4 tablespoons of boiling water (or more as needed) with the machine running, to lighten the texture. Throw in the parsley and stop the machine.

4 Pack the taramasalata into a china or toughened glass jar with a lid. Wrap in plastic wrap or a wet cloth for transporting.

5 Pack the blini, in stacks, in a cloth- or napkin-lined little basket or box for transporting. To serve, set out the blini, opened taramasalata and the opened 'saviar' with the remaining lemon half. Have knives or spoons ready for scooping and spreading.

Makes 48

Allow 3-4 blini, 1 oz (25g) taramasalata and 1 large teaspoon 'saviar' per person for an appetiser; double this for a main course

Ingredients

Blini:
- 1$\frac{3}{4}$ cups (200g) strong white bread flour
- $\frac{1}{2}$ cup (50g) buckwheat flour
- 1 teaspoon or $\frac{1}{2}$ sachet micronised, easyblend yeast
- 1 teaspoon sea salt flakes
- 1 cup (275ml) milk, warmed to approximately 99 degrees
- $\frac{3}{4}$ cup (150ml) soured cream
- 2 eggs, separated
- 6 tablespoons butter or olive oil, for cooking

Taramasalata:
- 4 tablespoons tarama (salted, pressed, cod's roe), or 4 oz) 100g salted, smoked cod's roe, skinned, chopped
- 2 thick slices white bread, wetted and squeezed dry
- 2 garlic cloves, crushed
- 1 lemon
- 1 cup (250ml) extra-virgin olive oil
- 3-4 tablespoons boiling water
- handful fresh parsley, chopped
- 4 oz (100g) pot 'saviar' (salmon 'caviar')

pa am tomaquet

In Catalonia, Spain, this famous and delicious snack seems as usual as pizza does in Naples. It consists of chunky bread, grilled, rubbed with a smashed garlic clove then with a crushed ripe tomato. Salt is usually added, but the final flourish is a generous libation of good, fresh extra-virgin olive oil: a tomato sandwich that is a triumph of simplicity. Create it on site using a portable barbecue, bread and plenty of fresh toppings.

Serves 4

Ingredients

4 chunks bread from a crusty country loaf
4 garlic cloves, skin on
4 large ripe, juicy tomatoes
sea salt
estate-bottled, extra-virgin olive oil,
    for drizzling

1 Take the gear needed for a fire on the spot: portable barbecue, gas-fired element or aromatic wood. Get the relevant equipment to the heated temperature or build the fire to hot and crackling. Toast the bread, both sides, over the heat.

2 Crush each garlic clove and use it to rub garlic all over one side of the toast. Now rub squashy tomato flesh over too; if it looks pink and messy: par for the course. Add salt to taste and a generous trickle of oil.

3 Eat each sandwich while warm, aromatic and crusty. You may add more salt and oil to the tomato debris and eat that too.

ewe's milk cheese on bruschetta

Long before bruschetta became fashionable everywhere it was a peasant dish from the Abruzzi, in Italy, designed to maximise the pleasure of tasting the new season's olive oil. *Fettunta* is the Tuscan version. Chunks of homely bread are toasted or chargrilled briefly then rubbed with garlic and sprinkled lavishly with the best olive oil available. In this version, pecorino is added. Some wild greens – cress, rocket or wild garlic leaves – can also be added. A portable mini-feast, all of its own.

1 On site, fire up a portable barbecue, make a small wood fire (if it is safe) or heat a gas-fired element. Barbecue, toast or grill the bread on a rack over the heat.

2 Use the garlic to rub all over one side of the crusty bread, then drizzle on oil directly from the bottle, flask or can.

3 Add some slices of cheese and some wild herbs. (Note: Do rinse them thoroughly under some bottled spring water to clean them well.) Sprinkle with salt to taste.

4 To serve, hand around the ready-made open sandwiches.

Serves 4

Ingredients

4 thick slices Italian-style bread e.g. *pane integrale*
4 garlic cloves, squashed
cold, first-pressed extra-virgin olive oil, to taste
9 oz (250g) pecorino cheese or other ewe's milk cheese
wild, fresh herbs such as dandelion, radish, cress, arugula or wild garlic (optional)
sea salt

salmon-rice beignets in little gem leaves

Smoked salmon, cooked rice and eggs combine to make 'beignets', golden and puffy, to eat in the fingers, and easy to transport in back-pack or pannier bag. They are good cool rather than chilled. Fold each in little leaves before eating. *Shichimi togarashi* is a kind of Japanese seven-spice mix: go to an Asian deli for this and for *wasabi* powder, an alternative.

Makes 24, Serves 8

Ingredients

4^1/$_2$ oz (125g) smoked salmon, scissor-chopped
4^1/$_2$ oz (125g) cooked white or brown long grain rice or wild rice
6 scallions (spring onions), chopped
2 teaspoons *shichimi togarashi* seasoning or ^{1}/$_2$ teaspoon *wasabi* powder
3 tablespoons tomato juice
2 eggs, separated
sea salt and freshly ground black pepper
4 tablespoons extra-virgin olive oil
4 heads Little Gem (mini-romaine) lettuces
2 limes, quartered

1 Combine the smoked salmon, rice, scallions (spring onions), seasoning, tomato juice and egg yolks in a bowl, stirring with a fork. Do not mash.

2 In a small separate high-sided bowl, whisk the egg whites with a pinch of the salt to a stiff foam.

3 Fold this into the salmon-rice mixture with about 1 teaspoon of salt, and pepper to taste.

4 Heat 1 tablespoon of the oil in a non-stick or heavy-based frying pan. Spoon in 6 small portions (about a tablespoon each) of mixture. Reduce the heat to low. Cook until golden and crusty, 1^1/$_2$-2 minutes on each side. Test one: it must be cooked right through.

5 Repeat with more oil until you have finished the mixture (total of 4 batches). Cool the beignets to room temperature. Chill them if they are to travel far.

6 Pack the washed, whole lettuces separately, wrapped in wet kitchen paper with some ice cubes. Enclose in a plastic clip-top bag or box. Pack the cool beignets in another box.

7 To serve, wrap each beignet in a few lettuce leaves, squeeze a little lime juice over, and eat in your fingers.

mini game burgers with bacon

Delicious, gamey meat patties with juniper and Armagnac to accentuate the autumnal tastes. In France these are called *gaillettes* or *caillettes*, depending on the region. Just the thing for a day out!

1 Put the diced game into a non-reactive bowl. Reserve half the bacon; finely scissor-chop or grind (mince) the rest, and add to the bowl. Add the Armagnac and the herbs, onion and the seasonings. Marinate for 20 minutes, or several hours in the refrigerator.

2 Stir the ground (minced) meat, breadcrumbs, crushed juniper berries and the egg into the marinade. Mix well, kneading with clean hands to make a dense meat paste.

3 Stretch each reserved bacon slice using a knife blade and halve lengthwise. Divide the meat into 16 equal portions. Squeeze each portion tightly into a ball then flatten into a burger about 2 in (5cm) across. Wrap a bacon slice around the outer circumference. Hold it in place with a wooden toothpick (cocktail stick). Repeat until all are prepared.

4 Heat the oil in a large heavy-based or non-stick frying pan. Add the burgers and sauté over medium-high heat for 3–4 minutes on the first side, and 2–3 minutes on the second. The burgers should be slightly rosy inside, but if you prefer, cook them longer until *à point* (to your liking). Remove the toothpicks (cocktail sticks).

5 Serve hot, warm or cold (but not chilled) with scallions (spring onions) or salad leaves of the season. Eat using the fingers or with a knife and fork.

Makes 1³/₄ lb (800g), 16 burgers
Allow 2 burgers per serving as an appetiser

Ingredients

6¹/₂ oz (185g) boneless, skinless duck, boar or pheasant, in ¹/₂ in (1cm) cubes
9 oz (250g) smoked streaky bacon
4 tablespoons Armagnac
6 tablespoons chopped fresh herbs e.g. parsley, rosemary, thyme or oregano
1 small onion, finely chopped
salt and freshly ground black pepper
12 oz (350g) ground (minced) beef or veal
1 cup (50g) fresh breadcrumbs
2 teaspoons juniper berries, crushed
1 egg, beaten
2 tablespoons extra-virgin olive oil

MAIN COURSES

chicken fajitas with salad

Fajitas – traditionally made with strips of beef in a marinade – are made with wheat, not maize tortillas and are a favourite at any gathering. This cross-cultural version uses chicken. For a beach *parilla* (barbecue) for a crowd, make it simple. These fajitas are do-it-yourself: this makes it fun for all and not merely hard work for the cooks. The four-skewer system for holding the quickly-cooked chicken is foolproof: try it. There is no waiting as all the chicken is ready at the same time.

1 Mash the drained red beans in their can using a fork, either before you set out or on site, and adding the barbecue-tomato sauce to make a thick bean purée.

2 Put the mashed beans, guacamole, soured cream and the cheese in separate bowls or containers that can be passed around. Have the tortillas covered, in baskets or between cloths, near to the barbecue ready for being warmed and filled.

3 Make the coating for the chicken: mix the chopped fresh red chilli together with the tomato paste or tomatillo purée, mixing in the corn oil. Toss the chicken strips in the chilli mixture until coated. Line up 24 chicken strips in a parallel row. Using 2 long skewers, thread the strips on to the skewers like the rungs of a ladder: they can now be lifted as one unit.

4 Repeat with the remaining chicken strips and 2 more skewers. Set these 'chicken ladders' over the *parilla* (barbecue) and cook for 3–4 minutes on each side, until the chicken is firm and white inside.

5 To serve, pull out the skewers and let guests fill their tortillas with chicken, cilantro (coriander) and the accompaniments of their choice. Squeeze a little lime juice over.

Serves 8

Ingredients

1 lb (450g) can red beans, mashed
1 cup (250ml) barbecue-tomato sauce
2$\frac{1}{2}$ cups (500g) guacamole (see page 16) or bought
   guacamole
scant 2 cups (450ml) soured cream
2 cups (450g) low-fat soft cheese, crumbled
   or sliced
16 wheat flour tortillas
2 teaspoons fresh red chilli, sliced
6 tablespoons sun-dried tomato paste or tomatillo
   purée
4 tablespoons corn oil
8 boneless chicken breast halves (breasts), sliced
   lengthwise into 6
1 large handful fresh cilantro (coriander) leaves
4 fresh limes, in chunky pieces

roasted sweetcorn and spiced butter

Mexico taught me to appreciate sweetcorn and its potential. Roasting or barbecuing it directly over the heat, still in its wetted husks, then sizzling it with spices makes this homely vegetable seem delectable, new and exciting.

1 Mix together the garlic, butter and paprika and set aside.

2 Gently pull open the green husks and silks a little and drip some cold water inside each cob – about 1 tablespoon will be enough for each. Set them over a prepared barbecue, 2–3 in (5–7.5cm) from the embers or closer.

3 Cook them over the heat, turning them with tongs or fingers from time to time, for 10–20 minutes or until steamy and semi-tender. Remove from the heat and pull the dampened husks and silks back completely to reveal the kernels.

4 Replace the corn cobs on the barbecue. As the kernels char and darken, add about a teaspoon of the spiced butter in little dots along the length of each cob. Let it melt and drip.

5 Once the corn cobs look frizzled and charred dark in patches, remove them and add a share of the remaining spiced butter. Eat, in the fingers, while still hot, leaving on the husks for holding.

Serves 8

Ingredients
3-4 garlic cloves, crushed
$1/4$ cup (50g) salted butter, softened
2 teaspoons smoky paprika, Spanish-style
8 whole sweetcorn cobs, husks and silks still intact

skewered shrimp with harissa

Harissa and herb butter make these jumbo shrimp (king prawns) on sticks very succulent and somewhat hot and spicy. If you cannot find raw shrimp (prawns) use ready-cooked ones instead: reheat rather than cook, using the same spicy butter, but for a shorter time.

1 Holding each prawn down flat on a cutting surface, use a sharp, serrated blade knife to cut the tail sections part-way through while leaving the head sections whole. The tail will divide into two, butterflying it. Discard the dark vein.

2 Mash the harissa with the flavoured butter. Use 1-2 teaspoons per prawn and coat the exposed tail surfaces of each. Thread the prawns in twos or fours on to long metal skewers, looping them round to fit as necessary.

3 Place the completed skewers over the glowing embers of the open fire, towards the cooler edge, or else rest them on a metal rack over the flames themselves. Once the shells turn rosy, brittle and aromatic and the flesh white and firm, they are cooked.

4 Serve the skewers with the remaining harissa butter in small pots, for individual use, and pass each diner a lemon half. Have lots of paper or cloth napkins for messy, spicy fingers. Toss the shells on to the fire with the lemon skins to burn to cinders. They continue to smell delicious and it also avoids messy clearing up at the end.

Serves 8

Ingredients
  16 (1-2kg) large shrimp (prawns) in the shell (about 7 in/18cm long)
  1/4 cup (50g) harissa spice paste (see page 43)
  1/4 cup (100g) garlic butter or parsley butter, softened (bought or made)
  4 lemons, cut in half, to serve

pit-cooked lobsters, shrimp & clams (clambake)

American summer clambakes are an old idea. The classic system, when at the beach, is to dig a pit in the sand, line it with stones, and build a fire in the pit. The food is placed on fine chicken-wire 'trays' which are lowered on to the hot stones, often between layers of wetted seaweed or samphire. The biggest foods go in first. As the steam works its way up it cooks the food to perfection. It does take some hours - this is all part of the fun. Have palmiers to nibble, soft drinks, beer, spritzers or white wine to drink until the main course is revealed. Get permission to build a fire if necessary.

1 Dig a pit 1 yard x 2½ ft (1 metre by 75cm) in area, and about 6-8 in (15-20cm) deep, in the sand. Line the base and sides of the pit with non-fracturing large stones. Make a fire with wooden kindling and charcoal in the pit and let it burn for 1-2 hours to heat the stones thoroughly. Have at least 2 pieces of fine chicken-wire cut slightly longer than the size of the pit, with the ends rolled to make 'handles' for lifting.

2 Kill each live lobster humanely: hold it down carefully, and pierce through the head with a sharp, heavy knife. Scrub the lobsters briefly in a bucket of sea or spring water.

3 When the stones are well heated and the fire has burned down, push the embers to one side. Place one chicken-wire 'tray' on the stones and cover with half the wetted samphire or seaweed. Place the lobsters on top with the sweet potatoes, onions (if used) and squash.

4 Add the second layer of chicken-wire then the clams, mussels and shrimp (prawns). Cover with the remaining wetted samphire or seaweed and a double layer of foil to act as a lid. Put large clean stones on top to keep the heat in.

5 Leave the clambake to cook for 2-3 hours or even longer. Uncover one side a little and test the food: it should be hot and cooked through.

6 Arrange the cooked food on several large platters, including the samphire, which is edible, and let the diners help themselves. Enjoy the foods dipped into the seasonings and then bowls of melted butter or olive oil. Lemons are an option.

Serves 8

Ingredients
8 x 1¼ lb (500g) live lobsters
wetted samphire or seaweed, to cook
4 sweet potatoes, unpeeled
4 onions, unpeeled (optional)
2 x 1¼ lb (500g) butternut squash, cut across into 2 in (5cm) slices
5 pints (2 quarts) clams, scrubbed
5 pints (2 quarts) fresh, live mussels, scrubbed
8 raw jumbo shrimp (prawns)
salt and freshly ground black pepper

To serve:
2½ cups (500g) salted butter, melted or 2½ cups (500ml) extra-virgin olive oil, to serve
lemons (optional)

barbecued red mullet with orange

'Woodcock of the sea' is one description of this pretty, pink, Mediterranean fish: it has a sea-fresh taste. If necessary substitute small red snapper or red bream instead. The orange, olive oil and anchovy add a Mediterranean touch.

1 Make 2 parallel slashes on both sides of each fish, on the diagonal.

2 Zest the orange into fine shreds. Squeeze the juice separately. Mix 2 teaspoons of this juice into the zest and stir in the anchovy to make a paste. Use this to rub into the slashes. Foil-wrap the prepared fish to take to the barbecue.

3 Put the remaining juice, the salt, pepper and oil into a screw-topped jar, to take separately. Pack a portable barbecue, coals and tongs for handling the fish, and the brine-packed leaves, drained.

4 Get the barbecue to the correct temperature: no flames; a steady heat; an even layer of ash over all.

5 Shake the dressing. Rub or brush a little over the fish. Barbecue them for 2-3 minutes on the first side; 1-2 minutes on the second: too long and they'll fall apart.

6 To serve, wrap each fish in two vine leaves. Drizzle a share of the remaining dressing over. Eat hot, using your fingers, and enjoy the livers: an epicure's treat.

Serves 4

Ingredients
4 red mullet (about 2 lb/900g total weight) scaled, gutted but with livers left intact
1 orange, scrubbed, dried
1 teaspoon anchovy paste or sauce or 2 salted anchovy fillets, mashed
$1/2$ teaspoon sea salt flakes
$1/2$ teaspoon peppercorns
2 tablespoons extra-virgin olive oil

To serve:
8 brine packed, or fresh, vine leaves

fennel with pastis

Cooking accentuates the aniseedy sweetness of this vegetable. The aromatics are also boosted by the liquor: both suit seafood of many kinds, including the Barbecued red mullet with orange (above).

1 Halve the fennel bulbs, lengthwise, twice each to give 8 pieces.

2 Rub or brush these using the salt, pepper, oil and liquor mixed.

3 Cook the fennel over glowing charcoal for 4-5 minutes each side or until wilted, fragrant and caramelised.

4 Serve with leftover marinade and a sprinkle of the herbs.

Serves 4

Ingredients
2 large heads fennel, scrubbed
$1/2$ teaspoon sea salt flakes
freshly ground black pepper
3 tablespoons extra-virgin olive oil
1 tablespoon pastis (or aquavit or ouzo)
scissor-snipped fennel tops, dill or tarragon

flower pot chicken

A friend, whose city garden has no space for a formal barbecue, intrigued me by barbecuing on his front steps: cooking food on a metal grill set over glowing charcoal, arranged on broken bricks inside a large earthenware flower pot, about 18 in (45cm) across. Ingenious – however, any barbecue will do.

1 Pat the chicken dry. Make 2 shallow long cuts in the thickest parts of the chicken so it will cook evenly.

2 Mix together the sauce, olive oil, lemon zest, lemon juice and juniper berries. Rub this over the chicken in a shallow, non-reactive dish, turning the pieces to coat them.

3 Get the flower-pot barbecue to the right heat. Set the chicken, skin-side down, and cook over a moderate heat for 6–8 minutes each side or until the chicken is firm, white and the juices run clear and golden, not pink.

4 Serve hot. Eat in the fingers or using a knife and fork.

Serves 8

Ingredients

8 small boneless chicken breast halves (breasts)
1 tablespoon sweet chilli sauce (Chinese type)
2 tablespoons virgin olive oil
2 teaspoons finely shredded lemon zest
1 tablespoon freshly squeezed lemon juice
8 juniper berries, well crushed or chopped

chargrilled asparagus with gruyère cheese

A simply delicious way of cooking and serving asparagus in the open, this makes a great starter or an accompaniment to chicken or meat cooked over coals.

1 Snap off any tough stem bases and discard these. Using a sharp knife, make a criss-cross cut, 1 in (2.5cm) deep, up the base of each stem to let the heat penetrate better.

2 Drizzle enough of the infused oil over to lightly coat all the asparagus. Add seasonings which will stick to the oil.

3 Set the asparagus on a metal rack with a fine mesh so that the asparagus do not fall through. Barbecue or chargrill the asparagus for 3–5 minutes, turning it with tongs, or tipping the rack so that it rolls slightly.

4 Roll the spears close together and sprinkle over the cubed Gruyère. Cover the asparagus loosely with some foil or a pan lid. As soon as the cheese melts, serve the asparagus straight from the barbecue. Eat it using your fingers.

Serves 8

Ingredients

about 2 lb or 2 generous bunches (1kg) plump green asparagus
⅔ cup (150ml) basil-infused extra-virgin olive oil
sea salt flakes and freshly ground black pepper
9 oz (250g) Gruyère cheese in ½ in (1cm) cubes

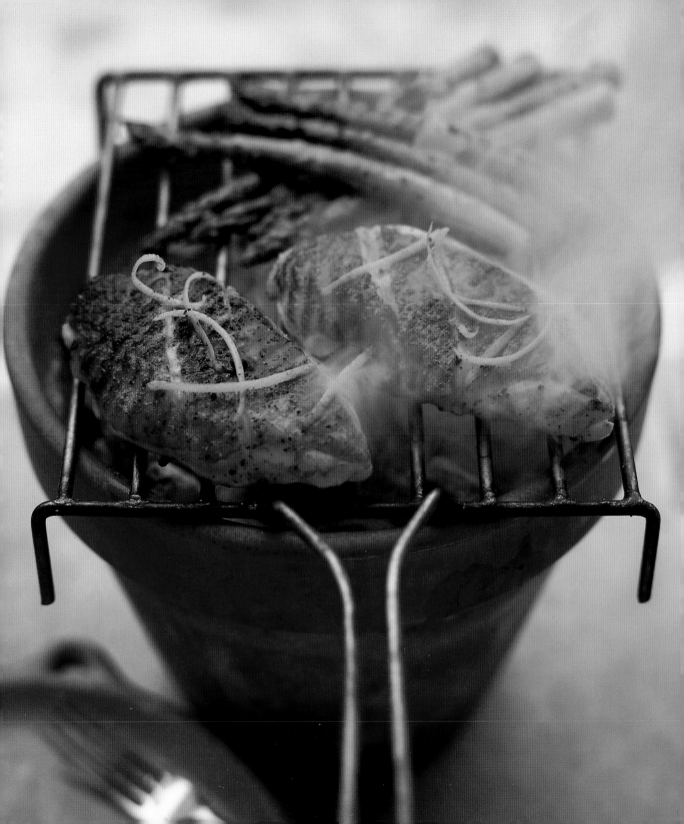

spatchcocked, barbecued quail with spiced plums

A perfect, crispy quail, cooked flat (spatchcocked) is easy to eat in the fingers at an informal barbecue. Spices, plums and a gamy glaze give distinctiveness to this easy game dish.

1 Scissor-snip up on each side of both birds' backbones then remove and discard the backbones.

2 Place the birds, skin sides up, each on its own sheet of heavy-duty aluminium foil. Pound hard to flatten the breast bones and turn both legs towards the centre. Cut a slash through both legs of each bird.

3 Mix the oil, garlic, salt, pepper, plum sauce (or jam) and half of the cinnamon. Pour some of this over each of the birds. Foil-wrap the quail, then plastic wrap as well.

4 Take the wrapped, marinated birds, the plums (sprinkled with the remaining spice), along with 6 skewers to the barbecue. Pack the salad leaves separately.

5 Prepare the barbecue: you should have ash covered glowing coals. Skewer the plums into one row using 2 skewers.

6 Unwrap the birds. Push 2 metal skewers, right to left, across two flattened birds, as if using a needle. Repeat with the other two birds. Drizzle any remaining marinade over the plums.

7 Cook for 6-8 minutes on the skin side and 2-3 minutes on the second, until firm-cooked. Add the plums when you turn them over. Remove the skewers. Serve on some salad leaves with the barbecued plums alongside.

Serves 4

Ingredients
4 prepared quail (each 6 oz/175g)
2 tablespoons extra-virgin olive oil
2 garlic cloves, crushed to a paste
1/2 teaspoon each of salt flakes and cracked
    peppercorns
2 tablespoons plum sauce, plum jam or
    pomegranate molasses
1 teaspoon ground cinnamon
4 red-skinned plums, halved, pitted

To serve:
crisp lettuce or chicory (witloof),
    or red trevise or radicchio leaves,
    or mixed salad

hot beef satays with herbs

These quick beef satays have a subtly sweet Asian savour. They take moments to prepare - a brief time to cook. Garnish them with fresh herbs at serving time, such as Thai basil or European basil.

1 Soak 16 short satay sticks or bamboo or wood skewers in water while the satay ingredients are prepared.

2 Mix together the first 7 ingredients to make the marinade. Thread equal amounts of beef cubes on the skewers. Set these on a shallow, non-reactive plate. Pour the marinade over. Turn the satays once and leave for at least 5 minutes.

3 Barbecue over glowing embers for about 2 minutes each side, basting with the marinade, until golden outside but still slightly rosy inside. Dip into the sauce and eat hot or cool, scattered with basil.

Variation
Substitute chicken breast for the steak, if you like; add $1/2$ teaspoon turmeric (optional) and use light soy sauce instead of dark.

Serves 8

Ingredients
4 tablespoons canned coconut milk
2 tablespoons dark soy sauce
1 tablespoon dark soft brown sugar
4 in (10cm) fresh lemongrass, thinly sliced crosswise
4 red or green bird's eye chillies, sliced
2 teaspoons freshly puréed garlic
2 teaspoons grated fresh root ginger
$1^{1}/2$ lb (675g) rump, sirloin or blade steak, in $1/2$ in (1cm) cubes
1 handful Thai basil or European basil, torn

skewered potatoes

An easy, tasty idea made simpler by having the baby new potatoes part-cooked before they are barbecued. The crusty, crunchy outsides are really tempting. If you can, cook the new season potatoes for this dish the day before the barbecue and refrigerate them.

1 Boil or steam the baby potatoes until barely cooked and still firm. Drain. Have at least 8 flat metal skewers ready. Push an equal number of potatoes on to each skewer.

2 Mix together the butter, oil, honey and half the scallions (spring onions). Dab or brush this all over the skewered potatoes. Cook them, at a reasonable distance from the heat source, for 3-5 minutes each side or until golden and crusty. It may take a little longer.

3 Sprinkle the remaining scallions (spring onions), the sea salt and pepper on top, and serve.

Serves 8

Ingredients
$4^{1}/2$ lb (2kg) new season baby potatoes, scrubbed
6 tbsp (75g) salted butter, softened
2 tablespoons extra-virgin olive oil
2 tablespoons clear honey
4 scallions (spring onions), finely chopped
sea salt flakes and roughly crushed black pepper

barbecued beefsteaks

Charcoal and beef steaks go together like bread and butter. The trick is to barely cook the meat at all: just sear and caramelise the exterior and keep the interior juicy, pink (or even 'blue') and wonderfully tender. Cook one steak per person or else buy a very large, thick steak then slice it into pieces for the guests. Using rubs, marinades and seasoning pastes adds lots of interesting tastes; apply them at cooking time or up to one hour before: too long and valuable juices will be leached out and lost. Buy the best steak you can afford: matured steaks from beef (not dairy) cattle.

1 Rub, brush or spread some of the selected flavouring on both sides of each steak. Ideally this is best done 10-20 minutes before cooking.

2 Enclose steaks in some oiled foil and twist ends up to create a package. Take them to the barbecue in this pack. Take some extra foil.

3 Have the barbecue prepared: glowing coals with grey ash on top, and set the rack about $1^1/_4$-$1^1/_2$ in (3-4 cm) above the heat source.

4 Remove each steak, using tongs, and set on the rack. Cook for 2 minutes or until dark and aromatic; turn and cook on the second side for the same time. Cook the large steak for 3-4 minutes each side.

5 Move the steaks to one side away from the heat. Cover them with fresh foil and leave to stand for 2 minutes.

6 Serve the steak with a drizzle of oil, salt and pepper and some scissor-snipped fresh herbs.

7 Some cold potato salad and baby salad leaves are great accompaniments, as is robust red wine.

Serves 4

2-4 tablespoons chosen rub, marinade or sprinkle (see page 42)
4 x 9-10 oz (250-300g) beef steaks cut $^3/_4$ in (2cm) thick; such as sirloin, rump or fillet (or 1 x $2^3/_4$ lbs/1.2 kilo rump steak cut $1^1/_4$ in/3cm thick)
cold, first-pressed olive oil, for drizzling
sea salt flakes and freshly ground black pepper
1 bunch fresh parsley, chervil or basil

marinades

Dry mixes, semi-dry pastes, sprinkles, rubs or liquid flavourants can add huge appeal to quickly-cooked meats, game, poultry or seafood. Even certain cheeses, vegetables and fruits can benefit. Since such concentrated mixtures may draw out too much natural juiciness, apply 10 minutes before – or up to 1 hour ahead – for best results. Some can be sprinkled or drizzled over after cooking.

bombay spice mix

Makes about 4½ oz (125g)

Ingredients
2 cinnamon sticks, crushed
2 tablespoons coriander seeds
1 tablespoon fenugreek seeds
½ oz (15g) dried crushed hot red chillies
1 tablespoon cloves
6-8 dried bay leaves, crumbled
¼ cup (50g) coarse salt crystals
2 teaspoons asafoetida powder (optional)
1 tablespoon nigella or black cumin seeds

1 Combine the first 6 ingredients in a *karai*, heavy iron pan or wok. Dry roast until aromatic, then cool.

2 Using a large pestle and mortar or an electric spice grinder, grind these to a powder, adding the salt towards the end.

3 Stir in the asafoetida powder and nigella seeds. (The asafoetida is optional but lends a pungency.) Store in a stoppered jar or pot.

Use in Indian dishes as a coating, a seasoning or a dry marinade. Also on lamb, chicken, veal, pork or beef grills, kebabs and meatballs.

peri peri wet mix

Makes about ⅔ cup (150ml)

Ingredients
2 tablespoons dried, or
    4 tablespoons fresh red bird's eye chillies, half crumbled or chopped, half left whole
4 garlic cloves, chopped
shredded zest and juice of 2 limes
7 tbsp (100ml) groundnut (peanut) or corn oil
1 teaspoon sea salt flakes

Pierce the whole chillies with a pin. Shake up all the ingredients in a pretty, stoppered glass jar or flask, ideally with a non-metal lid. Use as a marinade, to baste, or as a salad dressing. This adds a powerful hotness so use with care.

Baste shrimp (prawns), white fish steaks or cutlets, kebabs or whole small fish, slashed with this spicy liquid dressing. Drizzle it over cooked cutlets, fillets or steaks of salmon, tuna or swordfish. Sardines, herrings and smoked or plain mackerel also benefit from it.

provençal wet mix

Makes about ⅔ cup (150ml)

Ingredients
2 teaspoons sea salt flakes
3 garlic cloves, crushed, but left whole
7 tbsp (100ml) first cold-pressed extra-virgin olive oil
2 tbsp (30ml) red wine vinegar
2 stems (about 6 in/15cm total) fresh rosemary, bruised
8 fresh heads lavender, crumbled (or ½ teaspoon, dried)
3 in (7.5cm) strip fresh orange zest, crushed
8 fresh basil leaves, torn or chopped

Pound the garlic and salt together using a pestle and mortar to make a paste. Combine this with the remaining ingredients in a large sealable glass jar or a flask with a cork stopper. Shake well. Leave in a warm place. Use within 1 day.

Great for salads, for tenderising red meats and for use with roasted, cold chicken. Useful for pouring over grilled goat's cheese in a salad. Try also over grilled tomato halves, barbecued red and yellow bell peppers, chargrilled gaillettes (page 23) or lamb kebabs.

'ali berberé' mix

Makes about 4^1/$_2$ oz (125g)

Ingredients
2 tablespoons dried black
  peppercorns
2 tablespoons allspice berries
1 tablespoon whole cloves
2 tablespoons dried hot red chillies
2 in (5cm) piece cinnamon, crumbled
1 tablespoon coriander seeds
1 nutmeg, grated
20 green cardamom pods, crushed
2 teaspoons turmeric powder
2 teaspoons dried ginger

1 Put the peppercorns, allspice,
cloves, chillies, cinnamon and
coriander into a dry frying pan or
karai or wok. Heat briefly, stirring,
until they begin to smell aromatic.
Do not let them darken and scorch
or they will be bitter.

2 Tip them out of the pan and cool
them. Add the grated nutmeg, the
cardamoms, the turmeric and ginger.

3 Using a big mortar and pestle or
an electric spice grinder, pound or
grind the mixture to a coarse dry
powder. Cool.

Store in jars and use at an *al fresco*
meal – sprinkle it over barbecued
quails and poussins, spatchcocked
pigeons or guinea fowl joints. Use
on barbecued eggplant (aubergine)
chunks, carrot and parsnip halves or
fennel chunks. Add to couscous and
bulgur salads.

mexicana mix

Makes about 4 oz (100g)

Ingredients
2 tablespoons allspice berries
1 teaspoon dried oregano
2 teaspoons annatto powder or
  1 teaspoon saffron stigma
^{1}/$_2$ oz (15g) dried chipotle flesh
  (smoked, dried jalapeño), torn
  into tiny pieces
4 tablespoons mild or hot paprika
4 tablespoons piloncillo or soft
  dark brown sugar
1 tablespoon coarse salt crystals or
  kosher salt
1 teaspoon lemon pepper

1 Combine the allspice, oregano,
annatto powder and chipotle pieces
in a dry pan and dry roast briefly
over a gas flame or a barbecue. Do
not let them scorch, merely become
aromatic. Cool these.

2 Put the roasted spices, the
paprika, half of the sugar, all of the
salt and the lemon pepper into a
mortar and pestle (in Mexico it's a
basalt *molcahete* – perfect for this)
or electric spice grinder and pound
or grind to a gritty powder. Stir in
the remaining sugar.

3 Store in a stoppered bottle or
screw-top jar.

Try this with tortilla-wrapped
barbecued pumpkin, chicken, lamb
or some white cheeses. Sprinkle it
over avocado, red bean, chickpea or
blue cheese dips. Stir it into butter
as a baste.

harissa

Makes a scant 2 cups (450ml)

Ingredients
1 oz (30g) large, dried hot red
  chillies, crumbled
1 carrot, sliced
2 large red bell peppers, cored,
  deseeded, cubed
8 garlic cloves, crushed
1 teaspoon salt, or more to taste
2 tablespoons green cardamom
  pods to yield ^{1}/$_2$ teaspoon seeds
2 tablespoons each of cumin and
  coriander seeds
1 tablespoon black peppercorns
5 tbsp (75ml) extra-virgin olive oil

1 Cover the chillies, carrot and red
bell peppers in a medium saucepan,
with about 2 in (5cm) of boiling
water. Bring back to boiling, cover,
reduce to a simmer and cook for
15 minutes or until tender. Drain and
put the solids into a food processor.

2 In a mortar and pestle, pound the
garlic, salt, black cardamom seeds
(having discarded the seed pods),
the cumin and coriander seeds and
black peppercorns.

3 Add to the food processor with
^{2}/$_3$ of the olive oil and process to a
rough paste. Taste and add more
salt if necessary.

4 Pour the harissa into small, ideally
sterilised, jars, leaving ^{1}/$_2$ in (1cm)
headroom. Pour on the remaining
olive oil as a seal. Refrigerate.

Use to accompany barbecued
meats, fish, seafood or vegetables
also pasta, bean or grain dishes.

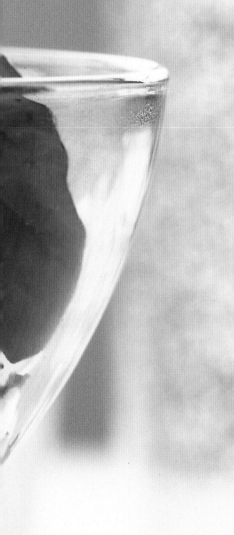

SALADS

potato & cheese salad

Easy, versatile, delicious: this salad can be served warm or cold made using whichever potatoes you choose. Some lively green leaves are added, as an edible garnish, at serving time.

Serves 8

Ingredients
2 lb (900g) smallish potatoes, scrubbed
salt
2 garlic cloves, crushed
1 1/2 cups (200g) soft blue cheese, such as Dolcelatte or Bleu de Bresse, cubed
1/2 cup (100g) fromage frais
4 tablespoons extra-virgin olive oil
2 tablespoons tarragon vinegar
crushed black peppercorns (optional)
handful salad leaves, e.g. red chard, nasturtium, spinach, dandelion or frisée, to garnish

1 Place the potatoes in a pan and barely cover with boiling water; add salt to taste. Cook, covered, for 16-20 minutes or until tender but still firm. Drain them well.

2 Turn off the heat and return them to the empty, dry pan. Cover the pan with a cloth and leave them for several minutes to dry out.

3 Meanwhile make the dressing: put the garlic, blue cheese, fromage frais, oil and vinegar into a blender or food processor. Blend or process to a creamy dressing, adding a splash of cold water if the consistency is too thick.

4 Cut the cooled potatoes into halves or quarters. Pack them into a portable container or clip-top bowl; sprinkle with some pepper, if you like. Pour the dressing over the top and seal the container.

5 Take the washed salad leaves separately in a sealed container. On site, mix the dressing in well or leave it as a topping. Toss the salad leaves on top. Serve the salad warm, or cool but not chilled.

pink, green and gold salad

Crisp beetroot and apple contrasts with the cabbage, spinach and sultanas. The sweet-sour effect is emphasised by a creamy dressing which turns pink when the salad is tossed.

Serves 4-6

Ingredients
4 raw beets (beetroot), scrubbed
1/2 head red cabbage, thinly sliced
2 red-skinned dessert apples, quartered, cored and sliced
4 oz (100g) golden sultanas
2 handfuls baby spinach leaves, washed, not dried

Dressing:
4 tablespoons freshly squeezed lemon juice
4 tablespoons extra-virgin olive oil
2 tablespoons clear, flower-scented honey
2 teaspoons caraway seeds, pan-toasted briefly
1 teaspoon sea salt flakes
1/2 teaspoon black peppercorns
2 garlic cloves, crushed
4 tablespoons strained Greek yogurt

1 Use a vegetable peeler to peel the raw beets (beetroot). Slice them into rounds, crosswise. Stack these and slice into batons. Put them into a portable salad bowl and add the sliced cabbage, sliced apples and sultanas.

2 Drizzle over 2 tablespoons of the lemon juice and 2 tablespoons of the oil. Toss until coated.

3 Put the remaining juice and oil, and all of the honey and the seeds into a dressing container like a screw-top jar.

4 Grind together the salt, pepper and garlic using a pestle and mortar. Stir this paste and the Greek yogurt into the dressing: it will turn creamy when shaken.

5 Take the spinach leaves in a sealed bag, along with the salad bowl and separate dressing, to the barbecue.

6 Toss the dressing into the salad until it turns pink, top with the spinach leaves, and serve.

rice noodle salad

A fresh, flavourful salad with both Thai and Vietnamese influences. Add the separately-cooked rare beef for avid omnivores and use fish sauce, but leave the salad free of meat and use light soy sauce for vegetarians: this salad works splendidly well both ways.

1 Pour boiling water over the dried rice noodles in a colander set in a large heatproof bowl. Leave for 3-4 minutes or until the noodles feel pliable. Drain.

2 Pour cold water over the noodles; leave 3-4 minutes or until cool but do not let them become soft. Drain well and return them to the empty bowl.

3 Add the next 6 ingredients; stir gently to mix.

4 Put 1 tablespoon of the peanut oil into a non-stick frying pan. Heat until very hot; add the steak, if using. Cook for 1-1½ minutes, turning, or until the outside is brown, the inside rare. Cool. Slice the steak into fine, ribbon-like, strips.

5 Combine the remaining peanut oil with the remaining ingredients. Shake well, pour over the salad and toss gently. Cover and leave to stand.

6 Take the salad in a snap-top container; wrap the beef and its juices in foil or plastic wrap. On site, divide the salad between the serving bowls; add strips of rare beef for those who like it, adding some of the juices as well. Serve cool.

Serves 8

Ingredients

9 oz (250g) dried wide rice noodles
½ cucumber, in julienne strips
1 mango, in ½ in (1cm) cubes or strips
2-3 birds' eye chillies, finely sliced
2 cups (100g) fresh cilantro (coriander) leaves, coarsely chopped
2 cups (100g) fresh mint leaves, coarsely chopped
2 in (5cm) chunk fresh root ginger, shredded
4 tablespoons peanut oil
14 oz (400g) slice rump steak, cut at least ¾ in (2cm) thick (optional)
4 garlic cloves, chopped or shredded
12 scallions (spring onions) or 1 red onion, sliced
1 tablespoon superfine (caster) sugar
2 tablespoons dark sesame oil
2 tablespoons fish sauce or light soy sauce
3-4 tablespoons rice vinegar
2 tablespoons roasted sesame seeds (optional)

DESSERTS

mixed fruits salad with passion fruit

A luscious, fresh fruit dessert that is vividly scented and colourful. Substitute seasonal fruits for any of those suggested. The essential, however, is the fresh passion fruit. Without these this is just a fruit salad. Remember that passion fruit – in their hard wrinkly shells – will keep for weeks in your refrigerator. Pomegranate molasses is a sharp, sweet, scented Middle Eastern condiment: look for it in ethnic grocers.

1 Scoop the flesh out of half of the passion fruit. Combine the flesh in a blender with the flower water and the pomegranate molasses or cassis. Give 8 or 10 short, sharp blitzes: you want to separate the seeds from the pulp to obtain an intense syrup.

2 Strain the pulp through a non-metal sieve and discard the seeds.

3 Select a beautiful, but portable deep dish or glass jug. Add the syrup, the remaining passion fruit, halved but otherwise intact, the peaches, figs, nectarines, cherries and the melon. Stir. Add the citrus juice. Stir gently.

4 Transport to the site and, to serve, let people help themselves.

Serves 8

Ingredients

12 fresh passion fruit (about 14oz–1 lb 7 oz/ 400–650g), washed and halved

1/2 teaspoon orange flower, geranium or rose water

2 tablespoons pomegranate molasses or crème de cassis

5 medium (500g) fresh peaches, white- or yellow-fleshed, pitted and in chunks

4 fresh, ripe figs, green or black, halved lengthwise

4 ripe nectarines or red-fleshed plums, pitted and in chunks

1–1 1/2 cups (250g) cherries, still on the stalk

2 cups (250g) orange- or green-fleshed melon, seeded, in 2 in (5cm) chunks

juice of 4 minneolas, tangelos, tangerines or satsumas

munster with pears

Though unctuous and silky to eat and deceptively mild, the strong aroma of Munster is often enough to deter many a diner. It combines blissfully with ripe pears.

1 If your Munster is a little underripe, be bold: heat it, still paper-wrapped, in an oven preheated to 450°F (230°C) for 5 minutes or else use a microwave (700-850 watts) on High for 2 minutes. This acts as an accelerated ripening process. The effect is intense. Take the cheese to the barbecue just as it is. It will begin to trickle and run before too long.

2 Leave the stalks on the pears. Using an apple corer, push upwards from the base of each pear almost to the top stem area. Do not sever nor twist. At serving time, push down on the stem area and remove the core.

3 Unwrap the cheese just as you begin to eat. Leave the pears whole. Let your guests use knives or fingers to eat their 100% edible pear.

Serves 8

Ingredients
small Munster cheese (a washed-rind cheese from Alsace), about 8 oz (225g)
8 ripe but firm dessert pears

raspberry fool with meringues

This is an ingenious recipe. The 'impossible' meringue idea, from my sister Alison, works brilliantly and makes quick, foolproof meringues: 80-100 or so. These are small, crisp and can be stored, in airtight jars, for months. But if you'd prefer to use purchased meringues, this too is an option. The actual dessert is assembled pretty much on the spot: its crunch, softness, sweetness and sharpness is a pleasant paradox.

1 Combine the 5 meringue ingredients, in order, in a heatproof bowl standing in 1 in (2.5cm) of near-boiling water. Using an electric whisk or rotary beater, whisk continuously until the unpromising-looking mix forms a dense, glossy, stiff meringue which will keep its shape. Remove the bowl from the water.

2 Set some wetted non-stick paper on 2 large oven trays. Wet the surface of these again. Put the meringue into a piping-bag with a $^1/_2$ in (1cm) star tip (nozzle). Pipe 80-100 small, neat meringues. Bake at 250-275°F (130-140°C) for 1-1$^1/_4$ hours or until crisp.

3 Take half, or as many as you want, to the barbecue along with the berries, sugar and cream, in insulated containers. Take a bowl, too, in which to mash everything together.

4 On site, mash the berries and sugar roughly with a fork and trickle this purée into the cream, adding whole or smashed meringues at will. Dust with a little confectioners' (icing) sugar and serve in glasses, cups or platefuls.

Serves 8

Ingredients
'Impossible' meringues:
1$^1/_2$ cups (325g) superfine (caster) sugar
2 egg whites
1 teaspoon vanilla essence
1 teaspoon malt vinegar
4 tbsp (60ml) boiling water
Note: Makes 80-100 tiny meringues. Substitution: 8 oz (200g) bought meringues

Berry fool:
2 cups (350g) fresh raspberries
1 cup (50g) confectioners' (icing) sugar, plus extra for dusting
2 cups (450ml) heavy (double) cream, whipped or 2$^1/_2$ cups (600ml) extra-thick, heavy (double) cream

chocolate cream pots

Chocolate is a favourite with young and old and these are luxurious, indulgent desserts to finish off a perfect meal. Use chocolate with a high percentage of cocoa solids - the difference is amazing.

1 Put the cream and the chocolate into a large heatproof bowl and microwave (700-850 watts) on High for 2-2^1/$_2$ minutes, stirring occasionally, until melted. Alternatively, set it in a heatproof bowl over a pan of boiling water and stir until melted.

2 Fold in the mascarpone to obtain a marbled effect. Sift the confectioners' (icing) sugar and cinnamon together and stir into the chocolate mixture, then stir in the liqueur. Mix until creamy.

3 Spoon, pipe or smooth the chocolate cream into 8 small china or glass pots to be taken to the barbecue. Do not overfill them. Firm them up by placing them in the freezer for 20 minutes, or chill for several hours or overnight.

4 Pack the pots into a larger box with a lid, or wrap them securely in foil into one large packet. To serve, unwrap the pots, and put a little stack of fine wafers such as *crêpes à dentelles* or chocolate matchsticks beside each dessert.

Serves 8

Ingredients
2 tablespoons heavy (double) cream
7 oz (200g) dark (bitter) chocolate, broken into bits
^{1}/$_3$ cup (50g) confectioners' (icing) sugar
2 teaspoons ground cinnamon
4 tablespoons Amaretto di Saronno or Cointreau liqueur
1^3/$_4$ cups (400g) mascarpone

To serve:
1 box crisp wafers or chocolate matchsticks, to serve

flambéed peaches with cognac and cointreau

This delicious dessert complements a bonfire banquet perfectly. Use peaches that are bought fully ripe or - if not - ripen them in a warm place. This is a bold but messy dish but well worth the effort.

1 Halve the peaches by scoring around the circumference, twisting them and removing the pits. Heat the peach halves in 2 large frying pans over a corner of the fire (you may want to use old frying pans for this as the flames may discolour them slightly).

2 Tear or cut the oranges in half and squeeze the juice over the peaches; trickle the honey over. Add the orange halves to the pan, if you like, for extra flavour.

3 When the peaches are warmed through and juicy, warm a large metal ladle and half fill with cognac, then top up with triple sec. Stir to mix. Hold the ladle near the heat and carefully ignite the contents with a long match or taper. Pour it, still flaming, over the peaches. Spoon the peaches and their liquid into pretty dishes and eat immediately.

Serves 8

Ingredients
16 small or 8 large ripe, scented peaches (4 ^{1}/$_2$-6 ^{1}/$_2$ lb/2-3kg)
2 oranges
4-8 tablespoons clear honey
1 cup (250ml) cognac, or more to taste
1 cup (250ml) triple sec (Cointreau), or more to taste

DRINKS

elderflower tea

Ready-made elderflower syrup is available from delis, good grocers and even some supermarkets. Use it along with a delicate China tea and, if real elderflower is blooming, add some washed heads of flowers too.

Serves 8

Ingredients
4 cups (1 litre) boiling water
1/4 oz (10g) China tea, e.g. jasmine
2 tablespoons elderflower syrup or cordial
2 fresh elderflower heads, if in season

Use a heatproof glass jug, vacuum flask, whatever pleases you and suits the occasion. Pour the water over the tea, tied up in muslin or in a tea infuser, and leave to infuse for 5 minutes. Remove the tea 'bag' or infuser and pour in the syrup or cordial. To serve, push the flowerheads (rinsed in spring water) into the tea at serving time. Serve in small cups, goblets or tumblers.

Note:
If made double strength (using only 2 cups/500ml of boiling water) and poured over 2 cups (500ml) of ice cubes, this can become a chilled drink instead of a hot one.

scented tea with rum

Tea made with aromatics is very alluring. Use China, Indian or an exotic tea from Sri Lanka or Nepal. Vary the additions according to taste.

Serves 4-6

Ingredients
4 cups (1 litre) boiling water
1 cinnamon stick, crushed
4 cloves
6 green cardamom pods, crushed
3 in (7.5cm) strip of orange zest or 1 in (2.5cm) piece of fresh root ginger, bruised
1/4 oz (15g) tea leaves
2/3 cup (150ml) dark rum, ideally Stroh type
1 orange, pith removed, sliced into rounds

Pour the boiling water over the cinnamon, cloves, cardamom pods, bring back to the boil, cover, reduce heat to simmering. Simmer for 3-4 minutes. Put the zest and tea, in a tie of muslin with a string attached, or in a tea infuser, into a vacuum flask. Pour in the boiling spiced liquid, including all spices. Stopper the flask. Infuse for 5 minutes then remove the tea and zest. If taking to a barbecue, take along another flask of plain boiling water, and the rum in a separate bottle. To serve, pour the tea, and add slices of orange and a dash of rum to each serving of the hot spiced tea.

mint tea

Tunisian tea houses taught me how refreshing this hot, sweet tea can be. Don't stint on the fresh mint: it is crucial to its success.

Serves 8

Ingredients
4 cups (1 litre) boiling water
1/2 oz (15g) unfermented (green) tea
5 oz (150g) bunch fresh mint, ideally spearmint, lower stems discarded
16-24 sugar cubes (lumps) or 8 tablespoons superfine (caster) sugar
sliced lemon or lime, to decorate

Pour the boiling water over the tea, tied up in muslin or in a tea infuser, in a jug or vacuum flask, adding half of the mint. Crush and press the mint then seal and leave to infuse. To serve, add sugar to each cup, glass or goblet, and a share of the remaining mint. Crush the mint and pour the hot tea over. Decorate with sliced lemon or lime.

sun tea

This can be made in a jug of water, sitting in a sunny spot with some fragrant tea bags suspended in it. Result – a thirst-quencher, alcohol-free, of simplicity and merit.

Serves 8

Ingredients
6 good quality tea bags or ½ oz (15g) loose tea (tied in muslin or in a tea infuser) e.g. China or Indian, mixed red fruits or Japanese green tea
4 cups (1 litre) spring water, tap water or filtered water, at room temperature
ice cubes
handful of fresh mint, lovage, bergamot or lemon balm leaves
2-3 tablespoons lemonade, undiluted
1 lemon, 2 limes or 1 orange, sliced
iced sparkling water, ginger ale, tonic or even lemonade, to top up

Leave the tea to infuse in the water. This may take 30 minutes or 2 hours depending on the temperature, the type of tea and the situation. Stir occasionally. Strain. Pour into a flask or bottle. Take along the ice, fresh herbs, lemonade, citrus fruits, and the top-up liquid of your choice. To serve, on site, crush the herbs and sliced citrus in a big glass jug with the ice. Pour the sun tea over. Add the top-up liquid to taste. Drink cold.

coffee with calvados

'Calva' with or in coffee is a delightful French idea. Add sugar – or not – to this fragrant coffee, depending on your taste buds.

Serves 8

Ingredients
2½ cups (520ml) freshly made, hot coffee
8 sugar cubes (lumps) (optional)
½ cup (120ml) Calvados, apple brandy or apple jack

Transport the hot coffee in a vacuum jug or flask. Combine a share of hot coffee, some sugar, if liked, and some of Calvados in each demitasse coffee cup. Stir, sip and enjoy. Alternatively, serve the coffee as is, taking along 8 tiny shot glasses. Serve a shot of Calvados per person in each glass, as an additional pleasure.

This indulgent drink is delicious when poured over scoops of frozen vanilla ice cream – a sort of frothy *affogato* is the result: a lovely dessert. (Keep ice cream cold by wrapping it in five or six layers of newspaper, then some heavy cloth. It will stay solid for 1 hour or so. Ideally, buy it near to the barbecue site, just before you start your meal.)

vanilla coffee

In Mexico, Café de Olla, an after-dinner drink, is sometimes served in big countrified earthenware pitchers. Adapt this idea for your own celebrations.

Serves 8

Ingredients
4 vanilla pods, sliced almost into halves, lengthwise
4 cups (1 litre) boiling water
4 teaspoons cloves, bruised
4 teaspoons allspice berries
1⅓ cups (200g) dark muscovado sugar
2 in (5cm) strip orange zest, bruised
8 cups (2 litres) freshly made cafétière coffee, e.g. Brazilian

1 Scrape out the seeds from the vanilla pods. In a saucepan, heat together the water, vanilla seeds, cloves, allspice and muscovado sugar for 5 minutes, stirring. Add the orange zest, crushing it well. Turn off the heat. Let it infuse 2 minutes. Remove the orange zest, and take this syrup to the barbecue in a vacuum flask, or in a heatproof jug that can be set on the grill.

2 To serve, reheat the syrup over the fire if necessary. Pour out some hot coffee into cups, mugs or glasses. Add a top-up of hot syrup. Pass around to your friends. Add half a cinnamon stick per person, too, if you like.

margaritas by the jugful

This Mexican creation is one of the world's most successful cocktails. More ice means more dilution; crushed ice will give a 'frozen margarita' – like a slush. Drunk *al fresco* it's usually easiest to shake the cocktail up with ice cubes. The salt rim is an essential.

Serves 8

Ingredients
- 1¹/₂ cups (350ml) gold or white tequila
- 1 cup (250ml) Cointreau or Grand Marnier
- 1¹/₂ cups (350ml) freshly squeezed lime juice
- fine sea salt, to decorate
- 8 lime wedges (optional)
- 2 cups (500ml) ice cubes or crushed ice

Pour the tequila, liqueur and lime juice into a large jug, shaker or flask. Seal. Shake vigorously. To serve, put the salt into a shallow saucer. Rub a lime wedge around each glass rim. Invert each glass in the salt to crust it. Shake off the excess. Drop these lime wedges into the glasses. Stir or shake the margarita up with the measured volume of ice cubes until very cold. (If using crushed ice, process in a blender.) Pour the cocktail into the jug; serve in the prepared glasses.

mint julep

To 'muddle' two ingredients means to gently mash and crush them using a long-handled spoon to extract the maximum flavour and aroma. Any long-handled, blunt implement will do.

Serves 4

Ingredients
- about 16 large, fresh mint sprigs
- 4 teaspoons superfine (caster) sugar
- 1¹/₄ cups (300ml) crushed ice
- 1¹/₄ cups (300ml) bourbon (rye whiskey)

Make these in 4 tall glasses. Put 3 sprigs of mint into the base of each. Add the sugar. 'Muddle' these well together to extract the flavours. Stir in some crushed ice and 'muddle' again. Pour in the bourbon (rye whiskey). Stir. Top up with extra crushed ice. Add the remaining mint to the glasses and serve.

Variations

mint-lime julep

Add a thick wedge of lime to the mint-sugar mix. Continue as above.

bitter mint-lime julep

To either of the drinks mentioned above add 2 shakes of Peychaud's or Angostura bitters to each glass. Do not stir. Leave as a 'blush'. Drink through straws.

applejack julep
Use applejack, Calvados or apple brandy in place of the bourbon (rye whiskey).

grown-up martini

Some martini aficionados merely pass the vermouth bottle, closed, over the top of the glass! Here is a recipe, rather stronger than usual, which is stirred, not shaken.

Serves 8

Ingredients
- 1¹/₂ cups (360ml) London dry gin
- 4 tbsp (60ml) dry vermouth
- 12-16 ice cubes
- 8 green olives (optional)
- 8 x 3 in (7.5cm) strips of lemon zest (optional)

Have the 8 glasses ready chilled: put them in the freezer for at least an hour or pack in an insulated bag full of ice. Stir the gin and vermouth together in a large jug over the ice cubes. Into each glass pour some martini. Drop in an olive or a lemon twist. Alternatively twist the lemon above each drink or rub the zest around the glass rim.

Variation

gin & it

Substitute dry red vermouth for the dry vermouth, but use equal quantities of gin and vermouth.